Creatures of Thirsty

Creatures
of
Thirsty

Payal Yagnik

2017
Xexoxial Editions
West Lima, Wisconsin

Designed & edited by mIEKAL aND
Cover art by Payal Yagnik
Back cover photograph by Susheel Dharia
Inside art by Aryav Srinivas

Some of these poems have previously been published in Danse Macabre Du Jour, Truck, The Delinquent, Quiet Shorts, Pirene Fountain, The Secrets Poets Society International Anthology, Forward Poetry

© Payal Yagnik 2017

ISBN-10 1-936687-34-8
ISBN-13 978-1-936687-34-3

published by

Xexoxial Editions
10375 County Highway Alphabet
La Farge, WI 54639

perspicacity@xexoxial.org
www.xexoxial.org

"Life and art are linked but it has to be fashionably done"

—Anonymous

Dedicated to my two lovely children, my kind parents, my loving grandmothers and all those experiences and relationships, fleeting or contrary, painful or ecstatic, that make me.

Exile

The fears move slightly to the right
inching onto crashing waves of resolute
four walls within four ears, deep trenches
lids within that fall slowly as early
autumn leaves receding horses of Benthos,
(October orange).
Dark slashes seduce time into November sunsets
hours lost within wantings and mustang branded .

Left palm under your right cheek, I sleep.
Your words locked inside my dead mouth.

Movements

Evening dog walks are like a stream of consciousness. The sun has just given up the day's fight and the gentle arms of the night are just enveloping me in a cradle hold. Its perimeter is vast, but I am covering only a short rectangle of existence. The dog marks this perimeter with ammonia as a catalyst, mobile and expansive.

It's late summer and a soft cool breeze is nudging my insides. A woman in tight black jeans hurries past. I thought she was wearing high heels but her speed contradicts this assumption. Her auburn hair glows as she passes the street lamp. I can smell it is freshly shampooed and virgin. Impetuously I want to yell out, "slow down sister."

A door clicks. A man steps on to the sidewalk and lights a cigarette. His stubble looks two days old. For a moment he considers both directions then starts walking left, towards us. His cigarette leads him on like a piper, its smoke following behind like a puppy, but it suddenly turns around and chases us for a good ten feet. I can smell his breath in that smoke. It won't kill me.

The Broadway side of the perimeter has a different haughty air about it. It is lined with perfectly spaced magnolia trees and beautiful lamps as if in complete submission of Ohm's Law. Not one bulb is flickering out of its last few breaths. As we turn a corner, the atmosphere changes. The magnolias have disappeared, so has the consistency of light. Half of the downward incline of the path is now lit by remnants of ambient light from the signs of the sushi pub shouting "WE ARE OPEN" and the other half argumentatively submits itself into a refined blackness. An imaginary line separates these thresholds as we cross them casually, unaware, every moment.

The only interesting thing that seems to leap out of this stillness as we encroach upon it, is the myriad shadows as they huddle quietly whispering like excited school girls. Suddenly a passing car makes them jump over the walls like scurrying lizards, expanding and blending. Somehow they seem more sincere and spontaneous in their theatrics than daytime clouds.

Love is a mad feeling. I bother explaining. A black woman is entering a house next door with a girlfriend. It is the only house in the block that hasn't been turned into a multiplex apartment. She turns towards me and as we briefly connect, I hear her speak "Who is she, I have never seen her, beautiful." It makes my heart smile. Strange woman, I think. She must have seen him in my eyes.

Fata Morgana

Painted her head stood smiling
nailed within the frame, scented
a garland hung dried and desolate
those languishing layers of dust
softening dark circles

I ran my fingers through
tracing her eyes
glint dimmed and dilated
as if their tired souls
escaped time in haste
amidst half-eaten meals

The bells of her earrings call out
urgent, like street-side hawkers
and deafen
I gargle her name
ritualistic
beads that bleed and string my being
in fated existence — Pray?

My looking glass shatters in that storm
her flowery curls wet when wild, punish
I smell rainforests
as the rains smell me

The room spins like a tornado
gutting my insides
her cyanide bleeds the sky

that night
all night
I sketched,
my quivering pencil of carbon
and flesh transient
in hope's substrate

And while her face changed with every blink,
her eyes stood still, very still

She is vacuous now
I must be indifferent then

The Burning Martini

Fingers curl a stinger
of scorpius   cherry nail-polish
and rumors   loud as they laugh
private in corner seats   voices to gain
precedence over words, eventually
Intelligent twists in shakes
of martinis and napkin stains
of prolonged drool drops   Stop mid-sentence
Eye blue upon eye green
blotting lipstick   from red to pink
dab the blush   hush   I hear nothing
The moving lips   the open lap
1.3 degrees across   her spandex in delicate overlap
that pivot of her line   she walks in stunted heels
a spinning platform   if only   you could cross
I order a bourbon, raging hot
and some lobster for texture
Spoons clash with glass   so often
like marriages that crash   so often
Forks lancing through flesh
and darting tongues through souls
Teflon they banned   not her cling-wrap
Jealousy strikes   right around midnight
A black smoke rises to these eyes
and I drip   alone   the forked road
of mixed feelings and chocolate fetish
(a cold room melting   82% black)
All I see   and hear
    is her   or is it him?
    A raw serpent on potter's wheel?

Wish this head shrunk-wrapped inside
a matchbox frame and set itself
on fire   a prayer   (So often)
A brick tucked between my legs
that wedding song that freed itself
from depths   of gut and garter   sings
Moaning under the cubes   its reflection speaks
to the face on that spoon   that enters his tongue
        while she stirs a vortex
          mad in my drink.

Pass the Tabasco — 3 poems

Theorem of Hindsight

The implications of spiral staircases jutting out, beyond the membranes of my vision are preposterous. I deliberately ignored the red flags of existential gods and let the complacent bull of denial roar as smoothly as a uni-directional rolling pin of flatlines. Discrimination is a colorless truth that sits like a flea upon personalized and intricately woven fears. The blisters in these feet have gathered rust now, they look like aging flowers that fell gracefully, gliding like mutated ballerinas over scorching sidewalks. Where is the dividing line of liquor and love? Or life, with all its conceit and will-power, building and destroying sand sculptures every fortnight, much like a koan. The cat sleeps, tonight each claw a saber-tooth scratch of memories   a door involuntary   half slit.

Goosebumps and Close Shaves

The burden of ends hangs low, fast falling like an unexpected drop of blood. Catch a teardrop midway and let it linger. Its embers light up a forest fire of words. Stop talking. Your applauses are silent and the drop of your eyelids deafen. I am your spirit trapped, screaming mute. My song lies within the patterns of your mascara and the misleading crisscross of your lashes. Set me free, not just now, you will know when. An insatiable ball of yarn unwinds my fears, the earth of yearn throbs. Your voice tears through the glass chambers within my heart. I chip away, catching my reflection in the changing faces of hypocrisy. Don't call me, never call me back. But talk to me, talk back to me. Everything stopped when he sang, the black cat

entrapped within the walls of my eyes blotted and
expanded, filling me in its fierceness and consumption.

It's beautiful, the way his poetry skips through the
notes falling off this skin, like weightless snow
crystals. He is the magician, the great illusionist, the
great manipulator who barely divides fact from fiction,
wrong from right, cats from foxes, in an extended
heady poise. The chorus voices dictate within my head,
an involuntary interference of deep conditioning and
acceptance. Now the watchers have gathered. Throw me
a dime, I am a destitute in denial.

Katafronts and Placemats

There was a quizzical look in each pair of eyes. They
were scrutinizing eyes, seeking to rummage through
the chapters of your life perhaps to find the questions
they sought. They moved face to face, looking, dodging
confrontations, this was a very passive aggressive
effort. Human curiosity can be a full-time undervalued
occupation; Alex spent the next few minutes analyzing
the erratic actions of his lover and his deep-rooted
issues. It comforted him to know that he wasn't the
problem, but that his lover's reactions had been rash and
egotistical, if only Alex could make him see the injustice
and in a perfect world, have him accept it. Kiss and
make-up over soft-serve ice-cream. Alex's phone stood
tone deaf.

"Please give me as much information as you can,
correctly, so that you don't go to jail today. Your
bail is generously set at $1,000" she barked au fait
as she walked a smug walk in her pedantic high
heels crushing lives and hopes. Still dazed, Gonzales
struggled to draw his attention to the papers in

front of him. He had been smoking a joint when they caught him for possession. He threatened nobody, he was nobody but a mere liver disease, he had cussed relentlessly at cops few times, now it all made sense. Could he flip off the public defender? What was her compelling problem? She still had that inconspicuous but obvious band-aid hanging on her scars from her recent facelift. "Get a new heart, you cold bitch" yelled Gonzales's eyeballs in a singular piercing stare.

There was something raw about Grace's walk that made people's heads turn and pupils dilate. They invaded into her, their incisive gaze intruding into the large electrifying field around her and falling dead like insects on windshield, one by one. She looked past the vertical stack of moving bodies and headed straight for the most visible part of the sidewalk encircling the giant fountain. Her spine quickly aligned itself to the perpendicularity of the projectile water in Y axis, as she fixated her visual awareness to the expansive sky above her. There were dimensions, within each layer the clouds spiraling, dancing, converging and dispersing as delirious spirits. It was a continuum, a pale concentration, dissipating, seeking freedom in groups, their blurred arms extending to join hands like contorting acrobats, and gradually being swallowed by a mammoth mouth of blue emptiness. The ground shook spartan. Then arose a fool's orchestra in urbane borderlines.

Sometimes, even love requires a two step verification.

peripherae

If I could mend the tunes I would
nothing reduces or distracts misery from itself.
I do not suffer, when I am suffering becoming.
Every curve of this line is flat.
I haven't pulled up too close behind you, have I?
Your breath fulfills our odd distances.
I step out into the porch and let the gray sky engulf my night.
Like an agent provocateur it is, an intercourse of pain.

Every passing car, a dog bark, the clank of rusted metal, an escaping tune through an earphone, a cough, the late flight that isn't mine, bicycle bells, a rumble, a thunder, a screech, a cricket, a snarl, keys typed, an inbox announcement, a blink, a click of my spine, the gush of blood inside my veins, the out-pour inside, a stretch of indifference. Nothing shakes the skeleton of this emptiness.

I was not born to create, I was created to be born. My self is an anti-spiral, it is a constancy of an inert vision. It is caught within the tangles of this mind and the minds of men. It cannot free itself; because it is self defeating, much like being caught in a riptide. I await the waiting game. Much like a leper's skin, I can only birth immortality through an indeterminate process of unreplenishing loss.

A Birthday Dystopia

Sometimes I get that wicked feeling that time has been wait-listed in perpetuity. While this fragile bougainvillea of life, with all its purple veins and pathos exposed, hangs caught within the inseams of unpredictability.

No one welcomes change. Christine said that I was her star student today since I was the first to upgrade into a one fear for all sign-on mechanism. I had remembered to click refresh on my self replicating thoughts. I had flossed the gaps between reasoning and irrationality and smiled jubilant, rephrasing and redirecting each unexplained attack of events.

I hear the same words from different mouths again and again, they have different styles of speech, tone and breath spacing but they say the same damn thing. I ask God for a sign tonight. I also ask the signer for a God tonight. Thankfully the greatest good that comes from silence is self-gratification.

Tomorrow I shall celebrate an event that took place in the past. (Even the words I strum now are in the past as they appear in human sight and get themselves settled over this document like fixated shadows.) I have no memory of this event I celebrate, of my birth or death. I only fantasize, much like a wine glass that fantasizes of my lips.

Judy was cruising the Caribbean with the family over the holidays. It was turning out to be a great vacation. Then Meryl, her sister passes away on the last day of the cruise. A heart-attack. Perhaps Meryl had pre-witnessed her death and decided to spend her last moments happy as she moved on. Perhaps she felt that the way we bash up our hearts day-to-day existing like mutating corpses, demand we immunize ourselves to heart attacks and heart breaks. And ask that primordial question, what if we could all pick our moments of death and steer a certain ascertainment to it? A miracle of old beginnings and newer ends? Or perhaps a contemporary misunderstanding?

The Burdening Vertebrae

I swore by the collar of your bones, horizontal, to never have forgotten
as your faces lay etched, paired in mismatched cufflinks
like mats of unlaundered clothes, waiting afresh.

Asking
Why? Are? You? Holding your breath as you quench your throat?
Evolution, the race within species, stinks.
Should I be betting on the Death Head Moth's brutal end?
Or the over-rated Monarch's fate as it jumps to its death?
(Economics of survival by voracious multiplication, devious!)
Or perhaps,
I should analyze why squirrels adapted to snacking on stolen fish and garbage
and why the Blackbird cheated with a Robin, repeat infidel?
(Economics of survival by standard deviation, genius!)

I swore by the collar of your bones, horizontal, to never have heard
that betraying chamber music while the carousel spun, queuing clangs of hollowed bells,
while legless unicorns, pole-danced with poison goblets in arms, in alarm mille fleur.
Even today, those clanks of virgin tongues laugh, childlike
echoing within my hollow bones, this demolition derby

drying up the marrow inside.
Could have? Should have? Would have? But didn't!

I swore by the collar of your bones, vertical, my necktie
loosened, to never have watched
diamond patterned butterflies in crawl, or clap over
headless Pegasuses in show.
But the center faces changed, my pacta sunt
servanda stumbling, blurry promises in tow.

The confrontation of a gasp, the radioactive symmetry of quotes and the inverted conversation

I dangled myself from the sagging wires. It was a precise balance of intent, weather-proved. The rains had poured mouthfuls upon my face and I had strained hard to look, unblinking at its source. Umbrellas are such a sham. No two could walk within one, mismatched footings and shoulders that rub wet. Unless you face off, what point can we make in rage?

Have you studied a little child who dances in the rain? A skip in her feet, she sings, she twirls, one with the droplets, an intervention of fractal ribbons.
I am a watcher, a freak who holds the lightning within his chest. I convulse, as thunder announces its departure, my arrival at this shore, frightening.

Much like close shaves, the ripples between the yellow brows drag skin to skin, unstable. I am stretching my imagination like a comet rising, beyond this skull, it creaks and the more it fills, it moans it speaks it leaks of lost words and disappearing fingerprints. Within lies a labyrinthine weave of fiery relationships, diamond and gold rings, that worry their eyes of dreams and tenses. I held a burning rose to their throats and they shriveled up, revealing bony breasts, a jardinière of rehearsed poetry.

The font of his thoughts read pale. The light and dark conjectures seemed to blend in to the warmth of a saki. I turned the pages of his mind and again and again the same numbering of its end hangs unread. I didn't

want it to end, never, the tip of his nib raises a fine point
when no one is listening. Every writer, a masturbator.

He took the last strand of darkness and made kites
with it. They flowered. Any fulfillment seeks emptiness,
otherwise where is that invisible audience that plays
within my head, yours and his? Please check in at the
rusted doorways that need more than a kick, they need
a plunge within their mouths, a free fall, a dissipation
of pity and instruction.

Alone, a quiet truth speaks; it's a travesty, even insanity
has sanity within it.

It is a much needed disappearance especially when
simulation of senses and insensitivity is involved.
I am not within, but outside the within, within
the outside and in. I cannot explain, you seek my
silence in billboards hanging within time, space and
inconspicuous matters. You talk about privacy, when it
is my quiet suffering that screams within the pitfalls
of your breath or the hang-time of lost calls and
screenshots. I am not here to tell you how I suffer, or
how much I love, it is all a myth this life, cloud-like.

the now and misunderstood

On the bright side, this is a spoon song.
I didn't have to plug it into a dry mouth.
The moon hung half mast, a wet half bed.
Nitwits, they shrieked, within your eyes
like bats taken by surprise
as scholarly pupils dilated to a thin line
their jump ropes snaked through our struggles.

HANGING; both an art and a science.

Your smiling face, a spinning top of motions.
I puzzle over the arrangement of these petals.
How words fall, how often we fail
this long walk of an ant, delicate, desperate
your browned mole, a one-track nose ring
diamonds in violence,
a lost journey dotting a swarm
of innocence.

How the jasmine reminds in her breath
tempered with summer;
this beating universe, a loud mortuary of souls
foot trodden longings
our nibbled pistils of vocabulary
that funnel through the admonitions of tears,
verses in therapy.
How this off-keyed white lie
unites
a lassoed blend of precise coincidences.

Discreet mode, moods and mediums

My evening stroll overtakes your midnight run, perhaps you don't use your arms much to paddle through resistance. You see, it is the blind turn of moments that are critical.

Should I brown bag my beer tonight 'coz the neighbors might notice?

People without air conditioners hang out more in their patios, caching winds. And people without televisions tower up their shoe bills.

I have an internal notifier system, that I generously demote with unintelligence.

We have talked about the heat thrice already. It keeps coming up as an unresolved issue. I think what I really want to say is that I want to keep you from filling up my pauses. I don't want you to think. Thinking is the root of all our problems.

Everyone is a poet, unless proven otherwise. Everyone has something important to say, and more importantly, to be heard. They are shouting out from their half opened windows, through air-ducts, from their balconies and their verses come crashing like bird droppings over your laundered shirts smelling of the mountain mist and nicotine. Perhaps it will outdo your body odor.

I have a rule. Please don't talk to anyone unless you have a pressing crisis. It is your crisis that is a trigger

for their new-found love or new-found appreciation
for their mundane, scavenging existence. The laws
of relativity shine like gold buttons and the laws of
ignorance rain like rainbow confetti. I have dust-mops
of various propensities.

The clothesline sags under the weight of these 'cleansed
souls'. You have wrung your eyes off their tears and
hung them out to dry while carefully pegging their
eyelids upwards.

A curious summer insect walks along the perimeter
of your laptop screen like a three dimensional online
investigator in prowl. At least it has left your beer mug
alone. You are in power. You can free it or crush it, at
will.

Bored but Immortal

Clockwork medusa's prickly braids, of random access memory, trapped
in nervous hippocampus rage, pecked
by indifferent ravens dangling summer BBQ 'd flesh in beaks, synapsed
time elapsed; wedged between karmic flatlines and peaks, speak.
Flash images splatter like drool droppings, on crisp white linen bedsheets
of reverted umbrellas in transdifferentiation.
Remembrance by his association?

Web covered grey Bodhi trees look away from the light in permanent retreat,
in temporal fright, the sight of his-horror her-guise.
Garbled scandals in my head speak, in rapid translations, does it ring a bell yet?
Darkness and death captured in timeless radiocarbon hell, skip generations
dancing in intricately laced possibilities, within the pillowcased mind to recover
your dull lost memories, knotted; sarcophagus in wicked Maya's silk skirt, lured
within her lost notebook pages, escaping scribbles on your breast, meaning little then. Priceless.

Wipe out I say. Erase. This mapping in my brain! This metempsychosis! Skipping
over space borne bubbles through discarded bodies of dark times. But this hollowed stomach
hungers more. Backlight in black and white, flashback in zebra stripes.

like a tiny flashlight pushing limits through tiny
keyholes, of threats and regrets and more.
Countless tangrams of forbidden engrams, unraveled in
bored 2 am stillness, meaning little then. Priceless.

Immortal medusa's prickly braids, of random access
memory
walking the walk, talking the walk, through the
garbled voices in my head.
My high heeled footprints in reflection symmetry, argue
in vulgar fractions, relentless its dissection fallacy.
And my tired calloused feet. Oh, my tired calloused feet!
Pecked and softened by the philosopher's pumice stone,
stagger
mindlessly, ahead. Bored but immortal.

Repercussions

The temperature has suddenly dropped. My heart had a sinking feeling earlier today. I shut my eyes regularly between blinks. It is raining drops of fireflies. I see them in tequila shots. And inside feeding bottles. I could nurse, thinking of you.

The lightning has settled comfortably inside. All ramblings are now electric storms with distinguishable patterns of geometric borders. Let them letch and snarf up imperfections. I love blots and their intense faces of unknown.

Samuel stared at me a second longer than he should have. He was hugging his wife a minute ago. I was watching. She has been trying to lose weight. Later we hugged bidding goodbyes. It was a lifetime. I craved an emergency braking system.

This August has been rather beautiful. The sun has maintained its thermostat. The clouds have maintained their dignity. But the valleys, they have lost their meaning. Their vulgarity blinds. I want to splash them with flowers. I want to splash them with freedom. I want to splash them with red.

11.01 pm. Ritualistically, the freight train honks. The traffic has halted to lay a red carpet of rails. The sirens go off in the parked cars, in submission, in unison. A joint venture. A man screams at his woman. She grabs his keys and runs out. He screams even louder, but the train overrides, voices visceral or dead. And people stare.

Why do people stare? Yet have a problem making conversation inside elevators? I don't get it. I don't understand freight trains either. I would rather kiss when stuck inside a car.

Getting down is always easy. But it often leaves behind footprints of a dirty hangover.

Pleasantries

The drop was shrinking. Slow to the heat.
Gradually giving in, into itself.
The baby nursed itself to sleep.
Rubber breasts that drew more blood than milk.
We live in such fragile times today.
The wine glass breaks first in slips
drawing blood again, more mad energy.

The patio is barren, and watered daily.
A lone watchman watches from across the street.
6 floors underneath, I stare back,
waving silent hellos with palaver eyes.
No one stands on their terraces these days.
Their blinders drawn, shut. They drink inside.

Why does a 4 year old need makeup
and a 6 year old want to be sexy?

The mist of the water burns the obvious.
Perhaps we need to use our hands more often.
More often, our eyes lie.

The Browning of Colors

A complexity is stuck in quick sand.

It moans as it caroms.
Scrub its hands and edges
of dirt and teeth
of time, standing still
like talking etchings, it shields
from the shadow of tenses.
Life in circles. Be-longings.

Today I moved in rhyme
with the seas, jibing side to side.
It changed colors like me eloquent
green, brown and turquoise, running away.

My pivot leaning, I caught
pieces of me
surface in breech
like unwed corpse brides.

How do the waters swallow sound, her shells that trap any maelstroms inside?

Let me fly, withdrawn. I feel tight inside my skin, this mud not mine.

Perplexia

(The whisperings behind machines drone the opening mouths of life-cycles, panty-hoses that slip slightly revealing mounds of flesh and hands that gather ruffles, backward countings between winks and nostrils that refuse landing or defeat, that shift between breasts, one constellation, one concentration, of a stare, raising a bouquet of colorless breaths or the silence of broken dishes.)

Perplexia, parched and dry she hums, this earth maiden in peak of summer, moonwalking inside songs, a leg dangling out of a sprawled blanket, a basket full of blank cores and green apples, pulsating the adolescent smells and sounds she holds just so her chest doesn't rise to her stampede of lips.

Her nagging juice so sweet, so old, I want to throw up or wrap my old legs around its throat, bubbles in miniature flamingo coatings, like flakes of dead skin over black holes, suspended inside halfway houses, waiting for a convoy of needles and the catapult of sun in their eyes.

How is your Dad now?
She gathers up her colors, her purples, her bleaching creams, her stash of preserves, testing tubes, violin and packs a bag, a matchstick and a roadmap of tears that match falsetto
blue snakes on her rattling wrists.
But seldom leaves.

Vanitas Emergencia

I don't see a fly as an elephant.

I stand watching myself, being exploded
paralyzed I scream as they make small-talk.
        "How no one cares these days."
The corridors are interesting tunnels
like flowery trails inside a mandala maze
they shunt bodies, some moving some moving dead.
        "Do you need a blanket Sir?"

The curtains hang white, they listen long
with frail fingers on their lips
adding a second skin to the skin
silent as fruit-bowls of cotton.
The drops of blood on the floor
since yesterday, have bloomed mosaic as petals
viral, fluorescent in bed spread.

A displaced putto dances on his hospital bed like a
ceiling fan, winged.
"Don't touch my backpack, you fellas always poking
around" he snaps
 "this room is too cold, do something."
        Sir, this must be a SPA not an ER. Do you have
an address please?

On a scale of 1-10
Where is my pain?

The 5th Season

The pieces move away like a teasing lick of flames, just out of reach. The electric patterns speak, cloud to cloud, quiet as a still-life painting,
                    a spoonful of flowers.

These endless toes and fingers, in stripes stroke themselves to make music. Piano keys that move ghostlike over blinds, rise and fall, zeroes and ones. This body, a chamber of commerce, three stories tall and depths to unspecified gravity. We are one. In exhalation. Black to white.

You can flip my pages but you can't see the writing under my obituary.

June mangoes smell crisp when treated, tongues wiggling like a worm caught in hook and your big tungsten eyes capture my cries dropping like dead flies to filament.

A sun-dried morning, undefined shades where seasons fuse hand in hand, dangling their bare legs as vulgar subjects. Every now and then, every nerve like cast iron skin, every moment exploding a silence within itself.
Unknown   non-existent.

The Ballad of Mrs. T Minus Time

Meta sensations, like untouched caresses
as if someone follows too close, behind
blurry timelines with flickering passwords
violated but never broken.
The groan of the dawn in its yawns, pathological
this eastern sky is dark.
Then, just behind the mighty film of mystic mists
when, the oiled wicks were once lit, stiff their necks
the bells sang incessant and calm.

Unseasoned, the poacher winds tip toe west, modern
and silent
invading every thought onto those we were born and
into those we drown.
These infectious spider veins run dry through the
desert sands, deep
their golden footprints raising history's demons, again
and again.

(A goat caught in mud, the pregnant lioness will kill to
fill, in due time.)

Did you notice the blackbird has changed her tunes?
How decibels flatline through metal and bone?

The muffled language these spirits speak
spitting crumpled texts from old books, haven't I heard
you before?
Sobbing over your passing, like a timeless widow.

(Only a hungry gut knows no fear, no order.
Only the drifting mind heaves in high winds and
lowered eyes.)

Leaning against a lamppost, flickering an elder widow.
Her belly disproportionate to her mouth
an open sore, in tobacco choke-hold,
her fire dilated and disappeared
somewhere around the wrinkles in her thighs
that clench to satisfy a void and a cry.
While her only child
(lost
and never found)
within the stains inside our heads,
rocks side to side
singing nursery rhymes auld lang syne. Yesterday.

Geometry

The old buildings stand damp and weary against the backdrop of a crisp night sky. The planets are outlined. A cat gnarls. Dead end.
I am trying to refresh memories. My eyeballs rapid
I push harder through the outlines and spiral into a vortex. The drain was left open. It hurt once. It doesn't hurt anymore. It smells.
"The connection was reset." Images invade. Snapshots. Why do most species lie on their spines when dead? Looking upwards towards a heavily dressed cosmos? It burns.
I am looking up. Horizontal. I peel through the layers of dust and fog and limited foresight. There are too many levels to conquer. I am caught within my own video game.
The semi-colon is an important syntax. I demand respect. Poetry is what happens between a period and a comma, vertical.
There are domes but no round structures. Half a circle, is it half empty?
My head, wish it was a twist off. With a filtering mesh. A french braid parts my mind. My third eye is squint.
I am grinding my molars and I don't even know it.
My fingers automatic, reach out to gratify the itch. Chocolate.
She frisked my crevices at the airport. I noticed a new mole, yesterday.
A child is blowing bubbles. A white dress flutters in the wind blocking my view.
My toes are painted black. So are her pupils.

memento mori

Sorrow, around your sequinned rims and glass moons.
I have settled upside down, wretched and comical.
Fogs that settle silent and lick
that thick red stain around our lips
invading boundaries slow
and gradually close in, until I
smell their breath, salty.

Sorrow, over the clarity of eyes, the webbed thickets
of skies that once sparkled orange and chameleon
and departed; your stars now hang
posthumous on ceilings egg-white
and glow fluorescent
as nightlights
unspoken
inside our bedrooms dim,
sunken lullabies that chant continuous.
      'Quod fuimus, estis; quod sumus, vos eritis'

Those monsters once awake, now writhe
between pauses in their breath, now and then
they hide within screams, left ajar as lips frozen
in kiss, between thresholds of deaths.

The cosmos shatters like glass, dusk to dawn
capturing tiny butterflies of papyrus.
Rain
my spirit torn, antemortem. I awaken.

Hounds of Cacophony

Caterwaul of sparrows like school girl squibs.
Welding machines heat, sparks in flesh.
Drills of jackhammers, pulsating bleat.
Reversal of backhoes thick-skinned, beeping stone-deaf.
Planes descend gradually shrinking, gray clouds in exit.
Clanks of iron rods, violins bleeding time to death, pink purple hex.
Hammering of wood, in hollowed volumes, pounding its cello chest.
Cars whoosh, shrieking heads accelerate.
Footsteps follow, step by step, silently equated.
Dogs bark, lectures that babel, gag and gargle scruples.
TV cartoons in 1, 2, 3s drip paradiddles cursive or abused.
Waters gush through spouts, loud and clear elongated
Sirens and honks, blare and bare, some spit bubbles to spare.
Gusty winds, cold shadows tremble clothed in shred, threads.

And, the giant crane blue obedient.
Rotates its single arm, plaster and graffiti, hollowed chested.
Right to left, left to right, perhaps clockwise anti.
Conducting this mayhem mechanical.
Everyday deconstruction.

The Logic of Subchapter F

He wore his long overcoat, cream
white pants and shirt, stained with dirt and ketchup, contrasted
His black skin.
He walked with a certain air, in a certain jazz kind of way
dignified; in the middle of the road, that he owned, without guilt.
The crossroads of life, he looked left to right
at that busy intersection, in short sight, craving french fries, hungry.
That seemed too dark, burnt lonely soul,
abandoned soggy, what is left to right?
And yet, he carefully, looked each side
to make sure, he didn't get run over,
short-changing fair God on his side,
sauteed fungus, mayonnaise with mustard, fine.

His long overcoat, that insecure night
hung loose, like wings fluttering, threatening take-off
any minute.
The two dollars he had begged, craved a muffin now.
The French café looked forgiving, it didn't discriminate.
As long as you got money, who cared, poor or aged?
And he spoke rapidly, but clear
flashing gaps in his teeth, that divided
nations, over pompous religions.
"Your wallet, sir, sitting over there, I can take care of it, if you like."
Then he went about his way, sniggering, cell in his ears
chattering incessant, as his bills ran over,

Days, months and years,
in scrolls, he screamed

    "Can you hear me now?
    It has been a while
    since my teeth broke roll,
    my tongue salted, now pickled.
    Oh Lord, when will you shape,
    this last saliva, into wine, bitter."

when Betty died

A day old skin yellowed more than pale lips
tasting sweet and remains of nothing.
The layers of water, smeared with ink
she dabbed them with currants and sour greens
over slow setting eyes.
Under the magnolia tree shaded, black and white
the petals mellow as leaves, she waited and wept
broken shell like, amidst a scalding sidewalk.
She waited tarnished like an old lady with no name
but Betty sounding familiar.

The old glass factory, chimed like cracked bells on a
dancers feet.
Gulping mouthfuls of pain all day, across the street
dotted with homeless apparitions, that lurked
like unnamed letterboxes and deformed tattoos.
The white crow chirped.
Oh, the bricks and glass that reflected her whorls of age
and memory,
a gray garden painted with freckled pink flowers,
swaying gently as shadows on streets,
the languishing cobwebs adding fade and a fake hint of
dignity.

This outdated mass   part skin part glass part metal
everybody   wanted out.
                Declined their notional values   they
said.
                        Demented bloody nuisance
they yelled
collecting fingerprints and her children's approval.
Her fingers trembled as little tsunamis of sweat

around her palms, raged beveled and turbulent.
She waited.
Caressing each bottle each day and placing them
against her ears, her eyes inside their oculus. She
listened.
With intent, and unblinking before their indecent
burial;
like a caryatid their stories echoed and danced
like light against blurred ceilings and her soul lunatic
their laughter, cried.　　　　　Their heartbreaks,
murders, suicides
dangling from the parapet, dead like old pigeons.

Broken and aged, they smelled
　　　　　but　　　　　　　　were not empty.

　　　　　Listen young fools. How hollow are your
minds?
　　　　　They fill with blood and sugar, half full they
hold tunes and empty winds.
　　　　　Nudge and rattle, their pebbles, their skins and
hear them roar like lions behind labels.

 Narrow your lips — widen that gut of surprise.
　　　　　Pluck that petal of a dying flower, squeeze fear
　　　　　and lock its last breath
　　　　　in your voiceless throat that is parched. Water
its mud
　　　　　with crushed ice and ash.
Even gargoyles smile pretty before dying. Like their
mothers. (Betty said.)

Tea

3 p.m. She invited us to tea
She, me and Dali
Cloth napkins, patties, pound cake
Why not?
Good snacks, good company to partake
The pentagonal table
She, me on armless chairs.

    Dali sat pretty
In her ornate throne
Occupying two seats
Propped up on two pretty pink pillows,
How do you do?
How do you do?
Lovely day. Fine, thank you.

    Dali sat pretty
Her long blonde legs
Flirting with the wind,
Saying nothing
I felt the hint
Perhaps of her being
A tad haughty,
Between sips
Silence joined in
While we gave each other once-over
Each one wondering
What the other was thinking?
How quickly conjecture and judgment
Gatecrash in
It's bloody amazing!

So tell me about you, Dali
What's your story?

      But Dali sat pretty
In her ornate throne
Occupying two seats
Saying nothing, glazing.

'She' politely chipped in
Dali is related to royalty, you know
You must have heard
Of Bebe Bisque!
Bebe Bisque?
Was it a long time ago?
Yes, of course
She is very rare
I have had her
Since memory persists.

(Oh yes, I remember
"The Persistence of Memory")
Very revered, very rare,
So is she always this shy?
Well, it is the undisputed truth
Dali only speaks to me
And her best friend Peggy Woods
She is rather lonely
New place, new face, new fears
But you should see her
When I come home
She greets me like a mad puppy
In separation anxiety
And you should see her
When I can't fall asleep

She sings endearingly (in my ears)
"It's raining, it's pouring,
The old man is snoring,"
Dali would you like to sing?
Sing for our guest please?

    But Dali sat pretty
In her ornate throne
Occupying two seats
Saying nothing, glazing.

The tea cups started drying out, empty
I had had my fill,
Thank you much
I must take your leave.

    And yet, Dali sat very still
    Dali sat very scared
New face, new fears
In the car,
Indefinitely divided
Today's bizarre meet
I cranked up the windows
Spiked up the heat,
Admiring on my dashboard
My bobblehead Raggedy Ann
Anatomically correct, priceless
in separation anxiety
The two of us, bobbing
in wanton rhapsody
"Whatever will be, will be
You for me, for you, for me."

rage

rage, painted on the red canvas bared
finds itself in crashes of pushcarts or crinkled napkins,
wails of babies shortchanged for enlarged disagreements
or silent shaking of mouthless heads, caught within pin-holes of squeaky dolls
scrolls of rolled white lies neat and stacked, gaping with open drains
wherein hawkmoths breed, mutating life's nag and crawl deaf
the pumicing of dead skin or lathering of hope, back and forth, excites
as life languishes as an empty bag hanging on an empty chair,
stuffed cushions and moth bitten seats underneath where fear hides,
the pumping of air frantic into lungs abused, release their panic
as champagne corks freed, feed, lost in release from mental prisons
between laundry days and dusting of pillows against zipping traffic
of thoughts mono-chromatic in nuclear fission, confused
clicks of combination locks twist and turn fate's wheelbarrow, forward and backwards
find and replace, replace and delete, once again switching unresponsive gears
yet awaits, that red canvas with wailing faces hammered, still

lying eyes that beg a foster home, a bed of lids to rest
a month, week or day, at best
as weeping candles glow half naked half decent, into dreams
melted, rage burning like cobwebs forgotten around
diffused corners of hung canvases, a lingering manic scent, wet
pain and pus stick to cotton swabs occupied, within sterilized brains
emotions dabble in phrenic rants, like running footsteps scattered on diseased pages
erasing prints of indexed fingertips that snap, crackle and whorl, dripping mad red.

Recall

It is not the stillness of the night that creates
discomfort. It is also not the absence of shadows.
The mail inside the letterbox is aging. It will get better
as it sits and ferments. I am trying to keep cool as the
summer degree rises. Pink lemonade and ice cubes to
chew.
Someone hides behind clouds. It's not my denial or
optimism. My daughter wants to spot ships through her
binoculars as we ride by the bay. Even this car is rental.
His fingers first pretended to be a DJ. Then they tap
danced over the desk. These fingers are powerful shape-
shifters. I love necromancy. Show-off! He didn't hear a
thing.
I am a book collector. I like to touch them, smell them,
turn them over, inside-out and sigh. I wait for them to
age well too. They get better with dust in thrift stores.
Meanwhile the moisturizers run dry over my lips,
faster than yesterday. I thought I had managed to keep
the gray goblins at bay but they surprised me. This
morning, I woke up to find the Seven Dwarves (or was
it the Shoemaker's Imps) had managed to climb over my
ego and vanity and painted my scalp salt. I must have
passed out cold, last night.
My intuitions soar when I run low on sugar. I can easily
tell where I left my keys or my brassiere.
Today Marilyn looked like dehydrated mushroom. Yet,
she was walking with a youthful vigor I hadn't noticed
in years. She was on new medication.
I shut all the windows, air-tight like pickle canisters.
It drowns the outside world. Everything dies suddenly.
The vacuum of sound. The creepers of hope sag out-
stretched like depressed corners of a mouth. I break into
a grin.

Why they tamper with music and madness

I have a need. No, let me not shy away from the fact that I am needy. My needs start off like tiny sugar pops and swell up like deep-fried wantons. The guilt burns and sizzles, I guess it is a matter of deep marinade. I am beaming orange today.

Life is flitting by like swift screen shots or like your expedited reflection over tequila shots. "It is the sideview perspective that catches most of its nuances." Just now, I watched the clouds move in, just now, the skies are dehydrated and the stars bulge like eyes of starving children.

I read a lot about aliens. (No, it is not a biography.) And they keep finding forms to fit in our historical boilerplate of things. I don't get it. Like some puerile shadow-matching game that researchers seem to occupy themselves with instead of playing Sudoku during their coffee breaks. I would rather nurse a new cigar, puff a few gulps, cough violently and spend significant rumor about abduction, while facetiously dousing its burning lips.

It has been a few years since I talked about love. (I am torn between that and aliens.) Suddenly love abducts you, like hypnotic Celtic music and leaves you ravaged, probed and tossed, a hiker caught in an irrational blizzard within your heart. I wonder if scientists ever receive any funding for their top-down theories on love. Bah, they work strictly on the nuclearity of the mind, racists!

I hear voices. Wait, that was the television. (Phew!) No wait, that was not the television. It was mother calling me and leaving me instructions over the voicemail, then the landlord called, he was yelling that the kids were too loud, uncle called. Apparently I wasn't taking his calls, Grandma said that I left the gas on when I was uploading a new profile picture. I couldn't hear her too well. Grandma has been dead for a few days or decades. I use her passing often as an excuse to get out of annoying phone calls. I wish she wouldn't call me.

The transformed ficus has borne a million mad fruits this summer. Relentlessly, the vampire bats circle, divide and conquer, much like relationships. It is a beautiful daligram. I hear them screech and the violin replaces the voices. A distant local train screams its ritualistic intrusion, I am already traveling, right here on this patio. Movement is always a matter of perspective.

caesura in sight

6 bulbs in a weeping chandelier, only one lit,
the art gathers around to mourn,
a domestic digest of everyday sterility,
how human-like in clangor.
However,
the beveled 3-headed mirror gongs, differently:
you see,
you must warm up the whiskey,
sharpen the bow of the violin.
For the magnum of life brews
hot and cold and tepid,
churning out inmates
of desire and experiment
and in-between,
while the plague of nonsense
mortifies the weak.
All within us we weave
yet another fatal pollen of
paradox and conclusions.
You see,
we are Creatures of Thirsty,
sometimes we lose ourselves
only to find our self
in a giant pile-up of tilted shadows
or
a caravan of darkness passing, intermittently.

Recounting Diderot's Fallacy of the Ephemeral

What time is it now?
What time since you left with my timekeeper, my grandmother's sand,
since they deemed loneliness as some strange contrived persecution of self,
or since the pollen from the sun reduced to dust or the sad graffiti of our crawl?
My lone guitar thumps a rhythm of a gasping heart, a lost child in the woods of despair.
If these lungs held freedom, where would they end?
What would they envelope? Precipitate?
Even a cage breathes within a corsetry of death and the blowing off of an afternoon candle.
Oh sing me the poor girl's song, of fugitive dreams and lost earrings,
a fool's cry echoing within white seashells,
or simply yet.
Shatter me like porcelain rage,
swaddling your time,
for what is time, now
what is time nowhere?

case of urban proof of service or service of proof

Borders of eggshells. We tread broken daily, burnt in half-baked truths, symphonies of hurt and telltale theories, what is the point of it all? Scrambled words need endless sheepdogs. Where is the pagan proof of simplicity? If symbolism rules, do you see my fingers? A lion in the manger feeds my self interest. Self correction is a lazy coincidence of desire and inaction. When your tectonic plates move, mine hold in resistance, in a misunderstood extramarital affair. Surface touches only circle the navel concentric. It is existential foreplay, needing no approvals within your four corners. I succumb to premature drowning. I smile and let it happen.

I was obvious. In my semi-formal ways. A hint. Of humanity. Of sensuality. Of those that fled senses of comprehension. I existed, as that anomaly between formality and exuberance. I wasn't an echo, a hymn, or a blur of the night. An inspiration of the dead, a thread of embroidery, a blank wall. There is a sense of untouchability. An underlying sacredness, of an interior sanctum of perversions. Of loneliness. Of a possible mate. Of a possible completion. Yes, I existed. In a memory lapse of a widower, or the regret of an absurdity, I existed. Only as a proper noun. Unpronounceable, if so.

No, I do not watch the news. I do not apologize often. I do not wonder about trends and manifestos. I do not creep up like phallic shadows. I do not bend my own bitter business. I do not tame other people's ghosts. I do not soil within the swamps of human heart. I do not crumple paper and recycle minds. I do not curl my temper into cotton candy. I do not curb my love into another snowball effect. I do not weave my thoughts on elaborate looms of domino. It's complicated, these layers, like smooth eggnog over brandy. You may have met me, and missed me totally. Perhaps I got off the elevator at the wrong floor and laughed. It is always the wrong floor, while you knew which door to face. Or perhaps you wondered why my look made me exotic? It didn't. But you wore a leopard print dress with a long slit splitting personalities. Insidious. Wicked. I watched you get off. I watched you dissipate, like a black skirt of the alleys. A hint of fantasy.

If I have to talk about the human condition, the philosophy of thoughts or rationale, or why some are allergic to cats and peanuts, I must first mystify with redundancy. For there is magic of illusion and the magic of magic minus theorem of logic plus one. And if reality was only to be quantified in pinches, it would reduce minimalism to its minions. But I am much more. I am not my fashion or earrings, or a flash of legs or a sparkle of eyes, I am not my smile or my senility. I am more, much more, sometimes measured in tears, sometimes in smiles, tiny introductions.

I saw him just beyond my line of sight, just beyond my threshold of knowing, just beyond. He held a shrunk thought. I saw him there, standing, just beyond and smiling a smile beyond the curves of my lips. It was as if he had just crushed his burning cigar of impatience, strewing its ashes towards unknown coordinates of my being, a renegade.

"Marizzta, don't make it any more difficult than it is, you said you would move out by Tuesday." Dates, dates, dates can be sweet. Dates can qualify city streets and be sweet. Dates, I hate. Dates. Timelines and specifics, juggle ideologies into sweet trivia of zipcode specificity. Stop giving me numbers, unless they reek of nothingness. Dated unknowns.

You can't garnish everything with holy basil to make it special. Eventually it has to pass the smell test.

Authenticity is now a conscious act of breaking down hybrids into their lowest common multiple. While normalcy curls up like Escher's Wentelteefje in your lap, your annotated indifference is a burden you will have to carry through several keratinized ages.

I think there is this great conspiracy theory. I checked the time clock on my phone, my laptop, my microwave and my watch and they all matched. Who are you kidding?

A strand of hair hangs off a lamp shade, it is a perfect culmination of thought and movement, it holds its stand, it sways its extremities gently, it is rooted at a perfectly unwavering co-ordinate, waxing and waning just subtly enough, to play with your line of sight. Obvious and disappearing. Much like the frailty of life mocking the sinewy grasp of predictability or vice versa.

He made me laugh and I thought I had caught myself laughing, only I had just missed it as I laughed. I always knew paragliding within one's brain is a conscious step within each unconscious breath.

La Purga – The Cleansing

I sweat in swirls as pressure hangs from beams
like floating cobwebs
(This hip leans, it has supported many clouds ten
months each)
The room compresses, sanity squeezes her walls in
humility
The ceiling drops fast as fast, as water burns
Hold, hold harder, as bones stretch their horizontal
flanges
thick as rubber and contract in minute vibrations
The thought is jammed, I shake, shake like a silver
rattler
and fear trembles down my back, a habitual epilepsy in
circles

What is for dinner tonight?
(I did not answer the doorbell this afternoon. I think the
postman left a note)
Grandma died honey, she left you with negatives and an
earring
Worries stack up neat, cross section where stress
concentrates most
like colorful lego pieces, incompatible with each other
A child is complaining of an ear ache, I think of cancer
Death!
It's a hot summer day, I am cold
My pillow is a garden bench, my skin my sheet (I hand
washed them today)
Sleep was when I never had children, now I have my one
eye open

I turn to Eliot I stole from the library, (and some wine)
"Those who suffer the ecstasy of the animals, meaning Death"
Sexton passed away on November 9th, a day after my birthday

Organic is good they say, these days
Only I cannot afford bread, but wine is cheap
It buys me sanity in temporary refills
Coins nag this head, like an old lady with Tourette's in long necklaces
Again and again, the thoughts mutate and
stronger they get immune to rastafarians
It's a dreary world out there, damn
those who talk in their sleep, don't need bedtime stories
Look under, I exist, inside your foam mattress and silver linen
A bedbug never shies when you dream
Ever do you imagine?
Why my hands tremble slightly more than yesterday?
My skin wrinkles faster than peaches?

Stop talking to me, instead tell me fat lies
dunked in cookies and cream
My needs grumble like a cat left out
along the rinds of my belly, too long, and now they meet
Fasting cleanses, cause or not, I detox fundamentally
and that adulterant white foam enters my teeth
reaching inferno eyes and liquid lips
I have lost 1 inch 1 hunch, my animal instincts
ringing church gongs inside my mouth

and this hysteric soul's cries recycle
through countless bottles and cans
filling white linings of wastebaskets,
smoky eyes mugged clean white again

Tonight let me sleep, turning my back.

why does a prostitute buy lipstick

She felt the weight of a million corpses thrown over her. As if she had suddenly sunk in quicksand and the grounds had converged, right before her sterile screams could escape through the cracks of closure. But there were no cracks, no gaps, no fissures, no indentations, no irregularity, no aberrations, no vibrations, nothing. It was a deadbolt, the murder of sound. An extreme weight engulfed her body, which by now had graduated into an anamorphic paralytic state. A single blink sucking out mammoth amounts of prehistoric energy, if only she could tell if her eyes were open or shut. There is something utterly terrorizing about a mind that refuses to die and a body that refuses to obey.
It is perhaps more revolting to imagine a body that refuses to die and a mind that refuses to obey, for isn't death but a state of that very mind? Within her irises, the pupils dilated and recoiled in fear of their own reflection, her ear drums welling up with the silence of a simple thud of a severed head. One swift and sudden samurai-like blade had sliced through those senses with a killer precision, deft in its at-will termination and slow kosher-like bleed of memories and denial. The abstraction traveled like a master manipulator between her left and right nostrils, a mantra. Her throat had now grown a garden of cacti pecked by the pins of words that seemed to shuffle their defeat and dread, as they hitchhiked through the swanlike tunnel of her neck.

The background changed. The layers peeled themselves the yawning arms of twilight.

A trapped shadow was banging her hands against
the telescopic windows of a car submerged in water,
her abysmal mouth birthing bubbles exploding into
countless silver suns and she rapidly being sucked
through their dark craters, only to be swallowed by
a vortex so fast and so furious that she could see her
veins change colors and dry up. A bludgeoning fall,
spinning like the uncoordinated arms of a possessed
high voltage line intending to shatter its own tensile
strength by its dramatic entrance into some tangible
dimension, or like an au courant squid gushing out
from an artist's brush over a moving canvas, only
with delayed coincidence. A ground to just float over,
touching but not.

The tessellating slabs slide, rearranging themselves
beautifully like a withering and flowering chess board,
as the pieces move, parting the vastness of her universe,
that existed only within the shallow and profound
depths of her madness.

Music floats in, a forbidden enchantress in a long
white dress, beckoning her into the Gaussian noise
of eternal gray whales, drawing her in and out of a
veiled consciousness. The marble columns of her brain
collapse like a deck of minion human cards, changing
faces like exposed predators, fathers, husbands, sons,
mothers, daughters, sisters, lovers, teachers, neighbors,
liars, liars.

Suddenly but gradually, someone ignites her feet, they
burn slow in surrender, she feels her toes. The fire
spreads, slow and seductive in its mayhem, rising in

tempo like the orgasm of Saharan deserts, and then there is concord, a cartel of all that separates the mind the body the soul the breath the spirit the right the wrong the colors the blackness the significance the futility, like an in-differentiation of questions and sand grains, the pixels of her existence unite and coalesce like aging creases on air, weightless, and she writes on
....
she wrote in lipstick.

Oh I would write you a eulogy but I wrote you a love song

Don't conceal those breasts, escaping your fingers,
the songs of the beasts trapped within your teeth
I can't sleep, give me one piece
this life shatters like a solid sun 'neath my feet,
when the ghost of spirits sings, sing me my dream
Don't make up your mind, my heart in tatters
seeks the tone of your love, lost midway, in between
I can't sleep, give me one piece
this life fades like the face in the mirror
when the ghost of spirits sings, sing me my dream
Don't kiss these lips, separating your being
the righteous path of doom speaks, in hearsay
I can't sleep, hear him ache thick and thin
this life dies like that glitter god of the skin
nonsense
when the ghost of the spirits sings, sing me,
sing me, oh sing me, my remains.

The extraordinary minutia of being

It's a disease of the imperative, as blatant as vulgarity holding her skirt up and it imposes. The stray creature of my mind remains half submerged in mourning. If self pity is forbidden, what remains is the burning of the dead within this tongue. Life within me lashes out a tune of revolution that self-serves. I know nothing about the elusive future and yet I bastardize it or revel in its loss. How do I crack the code of my own extravagant programme, chatter diffuses this blessed confusion to conflict.

Paco thinks I must have a hard time dating men for I come across as intelligent. A huge no-brainer, perceived intelligence can be better than pepper spray. The burden of survival haunts like an everyday beggar visiting. What can I offer but my state of rejection and acceptance bagged up in random variable haste?

God is in the moment, the movement, the magic, and that pause in all of the below. Spare me the idiots and their timed idiosyncrasies about love and loss as a diversion from dissolution. This pot called life stirs itself to a whirlpool at dusk and then, at dawn break, swallows itself like a zen black widow. Equilibrium is the matching of one man's breaking point to another man's climax. I rebirth myself in your mind each day, each day a different man and each day, I die, a different woman in your imagined touch. I oscillate, like a rhythm. Hear. Here.

The ordinary number of the beast

And the heads spoke with their voices again. It was neo-avant garde they whispered. The fads of limelight dropping shadows of irony, a random splatter of smiles and laughter, the significant roulette of wrinkles, experience, necessity and compromise. When life sits like an arranged vase over a butcher's block, still and perfect, this manipulation of vocal chords can distort universal vibrations of chaos to a consortium of symphonies one would pay money for.

I saw a Ludlum book lie over a mutable bed of a homeless man, he smiled twice at me, once when I passed me, once when I passed him. Even the homeless stick together, like a pack of non-toxic crayons, for pacific sardines are passe.

Stephen Warren had quit working for the juice bar, they served no alcohol, no more. He was now a server at the Chinese restaurant. They did not judge recovering meth addicts as long as you asked no questions about goldfish or fortune cookies. Like cornstarch they all rise to a high.

I admire French artists and children. The French artists painted real women and children draw stick figures. They are both true to their character, a stripped down version of absolutes. The middle of black and white is not necessarily a grayscale.

If by 40, you have reached a full circle, that rotation of man around himself, you are already ahead in the existential race. How else do you smile that smile after an incredible birthing experience, your smile racing in a Porsche hitting zero to sixty in 3.7 seconds and that "finally" smile hearing your name being dysgenically pronounced over the speakers while waiting those widespread hours begging for food stamps?

When the shaking heads speak, listen. It involves a shutdown of the obvious, a gush of pixels and fragments, swirling leaves, a confluence, a face fallen in the sand, the trampling of thoughts, the death of stick figures that you won't understand, you won't understand at all, unless lost and nude, and disconnect.

visiting the Andalusian dog

There is a deep sense of conjugate sadness that enshrouds my mind like the incessant explosion of barking hounds. The internal intruder alert is a faltering river of footsteps towards an abyss. I don't need a bodily summary of counting daily death in its manifold manifestations. I am a retired precursor to all things transitory. I am the one who nailed the buddha on the sidewalk and I am the one who offers him a daily dollar of faith. Perhaps even you have wondered, in a fit of rage or erratic experiment, or perhaps out of the drudgery of predictable boredom, to randomly erase that demarcating line between rationality and madness as two separate streams of inbound and outbound thoughts, finally colliding into some novel fissionary idea within a rabbit hole? While a dark cloud of horror and dread lingers inside, as a faithful servant, imploding around equinoxes, I fantasize, dropping slow melting ice-cubes, foretelling their way into my drink as to how every evolution in public domain involves an equal and opposite momentum of regression. And how we cherry-pick our desperate justifications through either a grin or a tear, soaked in 40% in-toxicity.

invoking the summer's swallow's tail

I catch myself looking up often. It instantly creates
a gap within my lips, while I am fifth in my head,
focusing squint on distances within a state of emptiness
and that space that invades every nook and crevice
and pore of this wrinkling skin. I cannot swallow
rationality, but am open to a sub-lingual dissolve of
every belief system, and lovers. Thankfully, everyone
has left my line of vision and sound tonight. The radius
of my imagination is a vibrational play-field of light
and longings and an occasional suspension between the
two, a Daligram. Like an experienced marsupial I haunt
myself, letting that flea of despair settle deep within
folds of arguments and conclusions. The trajectory of
my journey spans an erratic hurl of a comet through
the resurrecting catastrophes within my brain. Like
a swirling shot trapped within a fuzzy shot-glass, a
concentrated awareness awaits an explosion, da capo.
I am stabbed from the behind.

Futility of life sits pretty like a colorful stir-stick
umbrella, fox-trotting an abyss, awaiting a push it
wants to slip into, with a hint of coquetry. If I am
intoxicated enough, how does it matter if I ululate and
wake up dead?

Shutdown

My mind abandoned, sits idle
An underground bar, smoked out of business
Barren, a padlock bastard hangs, from it
Rusty creepers crispy fried brown, spread and sing
Iron ballads in black and white, mourning melodies
Tiny pale dandelions sprout from crevices, premature
Veins empty that trap, moisture stirred with regrets neat
I have kicked, pulled its hair and spat
It bellows and rocks, side to side and stops, dead silent
Pointless it stares, into oblivion, as those creepers swallow
A pale bouquet of wild flowers
Making love, slow and cold, gloom untuned
Licking with tongues skeletal, greedily through
A keyhole stolen, that never existed.

S-T-A-G-N-A-N-T

Ruffles, hemmed
    between
        constants and variables
           dovetailed.
Forgotten stitches
    tingle
        on scar tissue
           caressed.
Giggling through
    tiny spouts, sprouts
        by light, by night
           bartending.
Paper kites
    in flight
        wrinkled loose
           within my skull, lull.

CREATURES OF THIRSTY by Payal Yagnik
Printed in the Autonomous Republic of Qazingulaza

www.ingramcontent.com/pod-product-compliance
Lightning Source LLC
Chambersburg PA
CBHW051701040426
42446CB00009B/1252